How to Become CARY GRANT

A Remarkable Life in Quotes and Remembrances

by Horace Martin Woodhouse

COPYRIGHT NOTICE

History Company books are available at special discounts for bulk purchases (shipping and handling charges apply). For more information, contact:

History Company LLC
www.historycompany.com
(800) 891-0466

Printed in the United States of America.

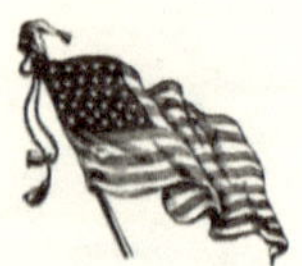

"Since I was tall, had black hair and white teeth, which I polished daily, I had all the semblance of what in those days was considered a leading man. I played in the kind of film where one was always polite and perfectly attired."

— Cary Grant

Words Speak Louder

Time magazine once called him "the world's most perfect male animal." Born in Bristol, England in 1904, Archibald Alexander Leach ran away from home at age 13 to join an acrobatic troupe as a stilt walker and juggler. Five years later, after touring with the troupe in the United States, he stayed on to pursue a stage career, appearing in several musicals on Broadway. By 1932, Archie Leach had become Cary Grant, cast as a leading man opposite Marlene Dietrich in *Blonde Venus.*

By the time he made *The Awful Truth* in 1937, he had invented a man-of-the-world, the epitome of sophistication, class, and refinement. In his words, "I pretended to be somebody I wanted to be and I finally became that person. Or he became me. Or we met at some point." Grant remained one of Hollywood's top box-office attractions for the next thirty years. Film critic Richard Schickel has called him "the best star actor there ever was in the movies."

This fizzy cocktail of a book lifts the veil off the debonair screen persona to reveal a real-life man full of inconsistencies and incongruities. It provides an unvarnished portrait of someone constantly in conflict – antic, serious, funny, poised, and a romantic who struggled in his own love life. You get a little history and a bit of sociology. But the most fun comes from an abundant helping of bon mots. His contemporaries as well as subsequent observers have plenty to say about the man who became Cary Grant. And his own undisguised words provide a sublime, truthful, and candid portrait of a curiously uncommon character.

Horace Martin Woodhouse

"Everybody wants to be Cary Grant.
Even I want to be Cary Grant."

— C.G

“Some actors squeeze a line to death.
Cary tickles it into life.”

— Michael Curtiz

"I have spent the greater part of my life fluctuating between Archie Leach and Cary Grant, unsure of each, suspecting each."

— C.G.

"Life typecasts us. Look at me. Do you think I would have chosen to look like this? I would have preferred to have played a leading man in life. I would have been Cary Grant."

— Alfred Hitchcock

"Hitch and I had a rapport and understanding deeper than words. He was a very agreeable human being, and we were very compatible.'"

— C.G.

"At any age, Cary Grant would still be a heart-breaker. He would still be the most attractive man on the screen. He did not age one bit. His hair got gray. That's all."

— Billy Wilder

"Do your job and demand your compensation – but in that order. It's important to know where you've come from so that you can know where you're going. I probably chose my profession because I was seeking approval, adulation, admiration and affection."

— C.G.

"He had poise, a great walk, everything women would like."

— Mae West

"I played a well-dressed, fairly sophisticated chap who is put into intolerable situations."

— C.G.

"He was conscious of body movement, like a dancer. It was wonderful to watch."

— Martha Scott

"You don't lose your identity up on the screen. It's always you."

— C.G

"One of the reasons he was so successful as an actor was that he truly just behaved like he was a normal guy and like he didn't look like that."

— George Cukor

"Ah, beware of snobbery; it is the unwelcome recognition of one`s own past failings."

— C.G

"He was very gentle and very dear with me. Working with him was a joy. There was something special, which is quite undefinable, about Cary. He was expressive and yet reserved. He was a quiet man basically, for somebody who dealt in comedy, and yet very much to the point."

— Audrey Hepburn

"Mostly, we have manufactured ladies – with the exception of Ingrid, Grace, Deborah and Audrey."

— C.G

[On Ingrid Bergman] "She wears no make-up and has big feet and peasant hips, yet women envy her ability to be herself."

— C.G.

"There are only seven movie stars in the world whose name alone will induce American bankers to lend money for movie productions, and the only woman on the list is Ingrid Bergman."

— C.G.

"His elegance, his wit, his true professionalism were outstanding, and I learned so much from just watching him work. The ability to ad-lib, the timing of a double-take, in fact, all his timing – so essential for true comedy."

— Deborah Kerr

"There was such an intense quality and focus about his work.... He was mesmerizing and very exciting .'"

— Alexis Smith

"He was extraordinarily sensitive. He watched out for himself, but never to the point where he stepped on anyone else. That's unusual."

— Loretta Young

"If you want to be an actor, my advice is to learn your lines and don't bump into the other actors."

— C.G.

"He made me feel as though I were the most interesting and witty person. He had that unique ability to make you feel as though you were the only person in the room."

— Elizabeth Taylor

"He was beyond any question the most attractive, charming, funny, sweet, marvelous man I've ever known.... and I haven't met his rival yet."

— Betty Furness

"He was the most fun and the most romantic man I've ever known."

— Mary Brian

"Dad was neither cheap nor excessive, which, for a wealthy man, is remarkable."

— Jennifer Grant

"I enjoy talking back and forth to people. You know, otherwise, I wouldn't get to meet the people."

— C.G.

"He was a thinking person. I had the feeling [he] wasn't primarily interested in money. His main concern was doing a good job. He was proud of his work.'"

— Seymour J. Gray

"He was a very sage person – almost like a prophet. A thinking man."

— Roderick Mann

"I'm opposed to actors taking sides in public and spouting spontaneously about love, religion, or politics. We aren't experts on those subjects."

— C.G.

"Nobody knows I'm a Republican. I don't make an issue of it because I have friends who are Democrats and Republicans."

— C.G.

"He was very proud that he had become an American. He was very patriotic, yet he remained very pro-British."

— Jerry D. Lewis

"Even though he was very pro-America, he was terribly British-minded. If it had anything to do with the queen or royalty, he was very upright about it."

— Binnie Barnes

"We have our factory, which is called a stage. We make a product, we color it, we title it and we ship it out in cans."

— C.G.

"And there I suddenly found my articulate self in a dazzling land of smiling, jostling people wearing and not wearing all sorts of costumes and doing all sorts of clever things. And that's when I knew – what other life could there be but that of an actor?"

— C.G.

"I think most of us become actors because we want affection, love and applause ."

— C.G.

"I tell you, in films, one doesn't really meet the audience. You don't get the impact or spirit of your audience, whereas when you are out in the public, you do."

— C.G.

"He was constantly a maverick, rebelling against what everybody expected him to do."

— Jack Haley, Jr.

"I wanted to live life, so I've tried to have a life and not walk around tripping on cables on sound stages."

— C.G..

"Cary is the most truly mysterious friend I have. A spooky Celt really, not an Englishman at all. He has great depressions and great heights when he seems about to take off for outer space."

— David Niven

[On his mother] "When I go to see her, the minute I get there I start clearing my throat."

— C.G.

"Autographs are ridiculous. When I sign one, it starts of a chain reaction. I'm not able to do anything else for the rest of the day."

— C.G.

"I regret.... the times when I was impatient with autograph hounds and pushy fans. I should have been more gracious."

— C.G.

"Chaplin has given great pleasure to millions of people, and I hope he returns to Hollywood. Personally, I don't think he is a Communist, but whatever his political affiliations, they are secondary to the fact that he is a great entertainer. We should not go off the deep end."

— C.G.

"My formula for living is quite simple. I get up in the morning and I go to bed at night. In between, I occupy myself as best I can."

— C.G.

"We should all just smell well and enjoy ourselves more."

— C.G.

[On Irene Dunne] "Her timing was marvelous. She was so good that she made comedy look easy. If she`d made it look as difficult as it really is, she would have won her Oscar."

— C.G.

[On Marilyn Monroe] "She seemed very shy, and I remember that when the studio workers would whistle at her, it seemed to embarrass her."

— C.G.

[On Grace Kelly] “She made acting look as easy as Frank Sinatra made singing appear.”

— C.G.

"Grace [Kelly] was astonishing. When you played a scene with her, she really listened. She was right there with you. She was Buddha-like in her concentration. She was like Garbo in that respect."

— C.G.

"We had a mutual respect for one another and shared some of the same philosophies. I got the impression that Cary had a great deal of love and reverence for life."

— Peggy Lee

[On Katharine Hepburn] "She was this slip of a woman and I never liked skinny women. But she had this thing, this air you might call it, the most totally magnetic women I'd ever seen, and probably ever seen since. You had to look at her, you had to listen to her. There was no escaping her."

— C.G.

"Cary was a lovely, very generous actor. A good comedian. And so funny. He had a wonderful laugh. When you looked at that face of his, it was full of a wonderful kind of laughter at the back of the eyes."

— Katherine Hepburn

"Cary was the best ham in the world. He had a wonderful sense of joy of the moment."

— Robert Wagner

"Cary had a real, solid humor, something so important and so rare."

— James Stewart

"He was a great one for jokes, and they were sort of risqué. It was a curious side of his personality."

— Gregory Peck

"Cary was an absolute delight to work with. Witty and wonderful, he entertained us by walking on his hands! But he was serious about his work."

— Jane Wyatt

"Enthusiasm was the most important ingredient in Cary's make-up."

— David Niven

"Cary was a subtle blend of elegance, sensitivity, poise, and charm, wrapped around a soul filled with wit, generosity, and concern for others."

— Albert Grimaldi

"He was as introspective and troubled as any sensitive person growing up in our society."

— Dan Melnick

"Cary worried, he was a worrier. He worked hard. I was very impressed in how prepared he was and how disciplined he was."

— Martin Landau

"The only really good thing about acting is that there's no heavy lifting."

— C.G.

"Cary liked women who had a distinction and a certain education about them."

— Leslie Caron

"All of my films were favorites in many ways. In one, I loved the director but not the leading lady. In another, it was the script but not the cast. Still another would be a box-office hit. An awful lot of stuff goes into the making of a film. If it all jells, then you've got a pretty good one."

— C.G.

"Hollywood is very much like a streetcar. Once a new star is made and comes aboard, an old is edged out of the rear exit. There's room for only so many and no more."

— C.G.

"I've often been accused by critics of being myself on-screen. But being oneself is more difficult than you'd suppose ."

— C.G.

"Adopt the true image of yourself, acquire technique to project it, and the public will give you its allegiance."

— C.G.

"My father used to say, 'Let them see you and not the suit. That should be secondary.'"

— C.G.

"*North by Northwest* isn't a film about what happens to Cary Grant, it's about what happens to his suit."

— Todd McEwen

[On Alfred Hitchcock] "Hitch and I had a rapport and understanding deeper than words. He was a very agreeable human being, and we were very compatible. I always went to work whistling when I worked with him because everything on the set was just as you envisioned it would be. Nothing ever went wrong. He was so incredibly well prepared. I never knew anyone as capable. He was a tasteful, intelligent, decent, and patient man who knew the actor's business as well as he knew his own."

— C.G.

"Cary is marvelous, you see. One doesn't direct Cary Grant, one simply puts him in front of a camera. And, you see, he enables the audience to identify with the main character. I mean by that, Cary Grant represents a man we know. He's not a stranger."

— Alfred Hitchcock

"[He] was probably the silver screen's most graceful man.... Nobody ever wore a suit quite like Cary Grant."

— Christopher Bray

"Men don't find me appealing, but Cary was attractive to everybody. Men wanted to look, dress, and be like him, but they couldn't."

— Peter Stone

"I don't dress for the moment."

— C.G.

"He turned down millions and millions of dollars when he refused to have a line of men's clothes. He said he didn't want to be the one who told people to wear something one year and throw everything out and start over the next."

— Bea Shaw

"If I want to wear short sleeves, I just roll them up."

— C.G.

"I consider him not only the most beautiful but the most beautifully dressed man in the world. His is a discerning eye, a meticulous sense of detail. He has the greatest fashion sense of any actor I've ever worked with."

— Edith Head

"Pride of new knowledge – including knowledge of clothes – continually adds to self-confidence."

— C.G.

"Other men wear suits. But with other men, there's the man and then there's the suit on him. That didn't happen to Cary Grant. For him, style was like a skin."

— Eva Marie Saint

"I eat whatever is put in front of me. I don't exercise. I don't have any hobbies. I don't smoke. I drink red wine. And sometimes I have one too many."

— C.G.

"Cary Grant at home was more or less the same man the public saw in movies: debonair, decent, and funny."

— Jennifer Grant

"Don't drink to excess, try to relax. Enjoy yourself and like who you are. If you do things in moderation, you're fine – except, of course, when making love."

— C.G.

"Cary wouldn't knock people openly, but he'd be very candid if you asked him specifically. He was smart, very level-headed, and perceptive."

— Marjorie Everett

"Cary was a singularly straightlaced and extremely correct fellow. He had a sense of kindness. If he didn't like somebody, he'd say so and then avoid them, but he didn't make a big deal of it."

— Irving Lazar

"I have no rapport with the new idols of the screen, and that includes Marlon Brando and his style of Method acting. It certainly includes Montgomery Clift and that God-awful James Dean. Some producer should cast all three of them in the same movie and let them duke it out. When they've finished each other off, James Stewart, Spencer Tracy and I will return and start making real movies again like we used to."

— C.B.

"Some people think that if they say something bad about someone, it makes them feel more important. In fact, it doesn't. It makes them more insignificant. People should say something good about others or keep it to themselves."

— C.G.

[On his accent] "It started because I was very conscious of my lack of education and I didn't want it to show, so I affected a sort of Oxford accent. It was an utter fake, a know-all who knew very little."

— C.G.

"I never associated him with being a working-class kid. I must say, I don't want to sound snobbish about it, but he never had any sort of Bristol accent. From the first time I met him, he always impressed me as the model gentleman. I thought he was Cary Grant off-screen, in real life. But that's what made him such a good actor."

— Peter Cadbury

"I think it's important to know where you've come from so that you can know where you're going."

— C.G

"If I can understand how I became who I am, I can use that to shape my life in the future. I want to live in reality. Dreams aren't for me."

— C.G

[On Douglas Fairbanks, Sr.] "He was a splendidly trained athlete and acrobat, affable and warmed by success and well-being.'"

— C.G.

[On Burt Reynolds] "As well as being my, and the world's favorite light comedian, Burt is a very considerate and thoughtful man."

— C.G.

"My screen persona is a combination of Jack Buchanan, Noel Coward and Rex Harrison. I pretended to be somebody I wanted to be, and, finally, I became that person. Or he became me."

— C.G

"[Grant] enjoyed being photographed."

— Everett Mattlin

"I'm no longer just the nice young man who knew how to put his hands in his pockets and smile broadly. I know the entertainment industry requires hard work, studies, determination and the drive for perfection, which one never achieves."

— C.G.

"In Cary's day you got nowhere – nowhere – with a lower-class accent and he was not about to be nothing ."

— Betsy Drake

"Actors today try to avoid comedy because if you write a comedy that's not a success, the lack of success is immediately apparent because the audience is not laughing. A comedy is a big risk. This is a tremendously costly business and to put money into a picture that might not come off – oh, that's pretty risky."

— C.G.

“Cary knew every facet of making a movie – a real moviemaker.”

— Cy Coleman

"It takes 500 small details to add up to one favorable impression."

— C.G.

"I can't portray Bing Crosby, I'm Cary Grant. I'm myself in that role. The most difficult thing is to be yourself – especially when you know it's going to be seen immediately by 300 million people."

— C.G.

"I tell you, in films, one doesn't really meet the audience. You don't get the impact or spirit of your audience, whereas when you are out in the public, you do."

— C.G.

[On *Arsenic and Old Lace*] "I was embarrassed doing it. I overplayed the character. It was a dreadful job for me.... Jimmy Stewart would have been much better in the film."

— C.G.

"I gravitated to men such as Hitchcock, George Stevens, George Cukor, Howard Hawks, Stanley Donen, and Leo McCarey. They understood me."

— C.G.

"I improve on misquotation."

— C.G.

"I can't make a speech. I am a rotten speech maker. Making speeches has never been my forte."

— C.G.

"We talked about life, food, paintings, collecting, about music — a wide range of things. He was a man full of curiosity. He was always drinking things in."

— Billy Wilder

"I was a self-centered bore until the age of forty. I didn't have time for reading. Now I'm reading, absorbing, listening, and learning about the world and myself. Understanding is as important to growth as patience is necessary to understanding. One must have perspective."

— C.G.

"Cary had a constant curiosity about everything. Life was a process and an adventure. There was always more to learn, which was certainly a lot different from the sort of current, popular, jaded boredom that one finds in a great many people who have had it all. It made him seem young to me."

— Judy Quine

"Cary kept notes on everything, including interesting words. Elegant words that meant something different. Words with meaning and sophistication. He wrote them down in a very fine, calligraphic longhand, in alphabetical order."

— Henry Gris

"He had absolutely no ego; he was just totally sweet and down-to-earth, and so funny. Cary not only had the best sense of humor, he also made you feel like you were the most important person in the world."

— Yvette Vickers

"The most memorable thing about Cary for me was his sense of joy."

— Peter Bogdanovich

"He thought too much publicity wasn't necessarily good for a star, that revealing your private life made you into someone average. He thought mystery was essential."

— Leslie Caron

"In private life he was a totally unsophisticated man. He didn't know zilch about wines. He didn't go to parties very much, and his idea of a great meal was sausage in an English pub."

— Roderick Mann

"The secret of comedy is doing it naturally under the most difficult circumstances. And film comedy is the most difficult of all. At least on stage you know right away if you're getting laughs or not. But making a movie, you have no way of knowing. So you try to time the thing for space and length and can only hope when it plays in the movie theaters months later that you have timed the thing right. It's difficult and it takes experience. I'll always remember the great actor, A.E. Matthews, who said on his death bed, 'Dying's tough – but not as tough as comedy."

— C.G.

“Even when he was having fun and laughing and making jokes, at which he was excellent, there was still a remoteness, there was still this keeping a secret.”

— Deborah Kerr

"He was so clever in not giving interviews and not talking about himself, never letting anyone penetrate."

— Jeanine Basinger

"When you talked to Cary, you never quite could get past the Cary Grant persona."

— Dina Merrill

"I have nothing against gays, I'm just not one myself."

— C.G.

"I have no plans to write an autobiography, I will leave that to others. I'm sure they will turn me into a homosexual or a Nazi spy or something else."

— C.G.

"I'm too busy living my life to write about it."

— C.G.

"Look at it this way, I've always tried to dress well. I've had some success in life. I've enjoyed my success and I include in that success some relationships with very special women. If someone wants to say I'm gay, what can I do? I think it's probably said about every man who's been known to do well with women. I don't let that sort of thing bother me. What matters to me is that I know who I am."

— C.G.

[On gossip] “I can’t control anyone’s thoughts. I have enough trouble controlling my own.”

— C.G.

[On unauthorized biographies] "They all repeat rumors that I'm a tightwad and that I'm homosexual. Now I don't feel either of those is an insult, but it is all nonsense. I don't care what they're saying. I've developed a skin like a rhino's."

— C.G.

"Dad somewhat enjoyed being called gay. He said it made women want to prove the assertion wrong."

— Jennifer Grant

"Cary wasn't a womanizer, but he loved women. He was always looking for one to make him happy."

— Binnie Barnes

"To succeed with the opposite sex, tell her you are impotent; she can't wait to disprove it."

— C.G

"I never knew any man that was in love with so many gals as Cary was."

— Hal Roach

"Cary's enthusiasm made him search for perfection in all things, particularly in the three that meant most to him: filmmaking, physical fitness, and women."

— David Niven

"I think making love is the best form of exercise."

— C.G.

[On Betsy Drake] "Betsy was a delightful comedienne, but I don't think Hollywood was ever really her milieu. She wanted to help humanity, to help others help themselves."

— C.G.

"For goodness sakes, why would I believe that Cary was homosexual when we were busy fucking? Maybe he was bisexual. He lived 43 years before he met me. I don't know what he did."

— Betsy Drake

"Most women are instinctively wiser and emotionally more mature than men. They know our insecurities. A man rushes about trying to prove himself. It takes him much longer to feel comfortable about getting married."

— C.G.

[On Virginia Cherrill] "My possessiveness and fear of losing her brought about the very condition I feared: the loss of her."

— C.G.

[On Barbara Hutton] "She wasn't cold to me. She was a lovely woman who suffered unjustly at the hands of the press. It was not her fault that she was born rich."

— C.G.

"I know they nicknamed us 'Cash and Cary,' but I never asked Barbara Hutton for a penny. I never married a woman for money, that's the God's truth. I may not have married for very sound reasons, but money was the least of them."

— C.G.

"He did not like my friends. When he came down and my friends were there he obviously didn't look amused. That upset me. It made me very nervous and that caused me to go under a doctor's care."

— Barbara Hutton

[On Barbara Harris] "Pretty good for an old geezer like me, isn't she?"

— C.G.

"He changed the way I dress, my choice of things, the way I wrote thank-you notes. He became my Svengali — he truly became my everything. But that's very dangerous, because it's like standing on a rug that anybody can pull out from under you at any moment."

— Dyan Cannon

[On women and marriage] "You marry them and they've got you. You have a child with them, and then it's completely over."

— C.G.

"My wives and I were never one.
We were competing."

— C.G.

[On his 5 marriages] "He went head-first into the affairs, throwing caution to the winds and quite convinced, in his boundless enthusiasm, that each romance was the one for which he had been put into the world."

— David Niven

"I was making the mistake of thinking that each of my wives was my mother, that there would never be a replacement once she left. I had even found myself being attracted to people who looked like my mother."

— C.G.

"I really expected him to make me happy. After all, he was Cary Grant."

— Dyan Cannon

"Cary never talked much about romances with famous women, but he did tell me he loved Sophia Loren."

— George Barrie

[On Sophia Loren] “He wanted to marry Sophia and would have if she had been available.”

— Frederique Jourdan

"I was fascinated with him, with his warmth, affection, intelligence, and his wonderfully dry, mischievous sense of humor."

— Sophia Loren

"Every one of my wives left me. I don't know why. Maybe they got bored, tired of me."

— C.G.

"It seems that each new marriage is more difficult to survive than the last one. I'm rather a fool for punishment – I keep going back for more, don't ask me why."

— C.G.

"Divorce is a game played by lawyers."

— C.G.

"We come into this world with nothing on our tape. We are computers, after all. The content of that tape is supplied by our mothers, mainly because our fathers are off hunting or shooting or working. Now the mother can teach only what she knows and many of these patterns of behavior are not good, but they're still passed on to the child. I came to the conclusion that I had to be reborn, to wipe clean the tape."

— C.G.

"I knew Cary Grant very well and he loved ... what did they call it? Acid! LSD. He said he liked to take the trip."

— Debbie Reynolds

"My intention in taking LSD was to make myself happy. A man would be a fool to take something that didn't make him happy. I took it with a group of men, one of whom was Aldous Huxley. We deceived ourselves by calling it therapy, but we were truly interested in how this chemical could help humanity. I found it a very enlightening experience, but it's like alcohol in one respect: a shot of brandy can save your life, but a bottle of brandy can kill you."

— C.G.

"The changes in Cary as a result of [LSD] treatment have been extraordinary. He's bloomed. He's lost his reticence and shyness. The barricade has been swept away.... and he's now free and spontaneous. He's got a freshness, an alertness, an awareness of things he never had before. Why, he's almost like a kid."

— Clifford Odets

"I am very close to Cary, but I just cannot understand why he keeps on with those crazy experiments, taking a drug to find himself. He ought to come up and see me now and then, and I'm sure I could quiet him down."

— Mae West

"There is a great misconception about LSD and a great deal to explain. I used it about 100 times before it became illegal. Each session lasted about six hours."

— C.G.

"I sometimes think Cary is attracted to LSD because those letters in England stand for pounds, shillings and pence."

— Alfred Hitchcock

"[On LSD] "I wanted to rid myself of all my hypocrisies. I wanted to work through the events of my childhood, my relationship with my parents and my former wives. I did not want to spend years in analysis."

— C.G.

"[It was] a most hazardous trip for Cary to have taken to find out what we could have told him anyway: that he had always been self -sufficient, that he had always been loved, and that he would continue to give a damn about himself – and particularly about others."

— David Niven

"LSD gave him the belief he had found the real answer to the miracle of how to live. Did I notice any real changes? Not really."

— Stanley Donen

"I didn't recognize that the changes in him were from taking LSD. Under LSD he was too placid. He was not his questioning self."

— Richard Brooks

"Everything was uncritical after LSD. It wasn't real. It was beatific. You'd say, 'Cary stop it. You're making me crazy.' He'd say, 'I'm not making you crazy. You're making you crazy.' It was cosmic in scope. Up and down. Black was white. In was out. Everything was a cycle. What's the difference? He could literally stop any discussion by one of these tautologies.'"

— Peter Stone

"I learned many things in the quiet of that room. I learned that everything is or becomes its own opposite. You know, we are all unconsciously holding our anus. In one LSD dream I imagined myself as a giant penis launching off from earth like a spaceship."

— C.G.

"Cary Grant was always my idol. When I was young I modeled myself on him.'"

— Timothy Leary

"I've been called the longest-lasting young man about town. It's ridiculous for a man in his fifties, but then until thirty-five a man is often a self-centered idiot. After thirty-five he should begin to make more sense. Sufficient kicks in the rear over the years do make a difference."

— C.G.

"When a young fellow like Louis Jourdan moves in on your field, you take stock of your assets and liabilities. It make you nervous."

— C.G.

"Can you imagine the wonderful parts he must have turned down in the last twenty years.'"

— Louis Jourdan

"For more than half of my 58 years, I have cautiously peered from behind the face of a man known as Cary Grant. The protection of that façade proved both an advantage and a disadvantage. If I couldn't see out, how could anybody see in?"

— C.G.

"His determination never to abandon the security of playing the character he had so carefully created for the screen made him unwilling to experiment or to display his extraordinary talent as a film actor in unexpected roles ."

— Geoffrey Wansell

[On retirement] "I got tired of getting up at six o'clock and tripping over all those cables and drinking out of Styrofoam cups. It's not as glamorous as you might think."

— C.G.

"Everyone tells me I've had such an interesting life, but sometimes I think it's been nothing but stomach disturbances and self-concern."

— C.G.

[On his daughter] "Jennifer is the best production I ever made."

— C.G.

"If I had known then what I know now, if I had not been so utterly stupid, I would have had a hundred children and I would have built a ranch to keep them on."

— C.G.

"Everyone grows old, except Cary Grant."

— Grace Kelly

[On aging] "When people tell you how young you look, they are also telling you how old you are."

— C.G.

"The older I get the more invitations come my way. I think people are just curious to see if I can still walk."

— C.G.

"There is no doubt I am aging. My format of comedy is still the same as ever. I gravitate toward scripts that put me in an untenable position. Then the rest of the picture is spent in trying to squirm out of it. Naturally, I always get the girl in the end. It may appear old-fashioned. There seems to be a trend toward satirical comedy, like *The Apartment.* Perhaps it is because young writers today feel satirical living in a world that seems headed for destruction."

— C.G.

"There's no point in being unhappy about growing older. Just think of the millions who have been denied the privilege."

— C.G.

[At age 60] “I don't like to see men of my age making love on the screen .”

— C.G.

"I'd like to have made one of those big splashy Technicolor musicals with Rita Hayworth."

— C.G.

"Preserving what is left is more important than mourning what is lost.'"

— C.G.

"I asked James Stewart recently if he had thought about dying. He said he hadn't at all. But I have."

— C.G.

[On dying] "I often wonder how I am going to do it. Do you ever wonder whether you are going to embarrass someone or do it in your sleep?"

— C.G.

"I would have thought that medical science would have had the problem of death all sorted out. I was sure that by the time I reached the age I am now, they would have found a cure for it, that they would be able to transplant everything and we'd all just keep right on going forever."

— C.G.

"There was a serenity about him at eighty.
He never became an old man."

— Peter Bogdanovich

"Cary had such a fertile, inquisitive mind.
And he never lost his almost militarylike walk.
He walked with authority right to the end."

— Bea Shaw

"I'd be a nut to go through all that again, but I wouldn't have missed it for anything."

— C.G.

"Even in the last minutes of his life, he looked better than most forty-year-olds."

— George Kennedy

"It was in keeping with Cary that he went quietly and quickly, without any prolonged period of illness. Nobody saw any pain or suffering or unpleasantness. He certainly wouldn't have liked that – to have people know that he was ill or incapacitated."

— Gregory Peck

"When he died, not only was Cary gone, but an era had disappeared.'"

— Fay Wray

"Style ends and begins with Cary Grant."

— Ralph Lauren

"I think that people like Cary who create work that lives have a kind of continuing presence."

— George Stevens, Jr.

"Cary Grant was one of the great people in show business. He was a consummate actor and a complete professional insofar as his work was concerned."

— James Stewart

"He was the most handsome, witty, and stylish leading man both on and off the screen. I adored him."

— Eva Marie Saint

“Grant is the only actor I ever truly loved.”

— Alfred Hitchcock

"He had the greatest gift, and that was the pleasure in his work. I can confess that I've been in love with him all my life."

— Celeste Holm

"I had a crush on Dad.... more than a little crush on Dad."

— Jennifer Grant

"I always thought and hoped that he was immortal. His innate dignity and grace enhanced everyone fortunate enough to be a member of the same profession."

— Jack Lemmon

"His life was lived with consummate grace.
He gave new meaning to the word gentleman
at a time when that word was out of fashion."

— Charlton Heston

"Most of the time when I remember something Cary said or did, I find myself smiling."

— Bea Shaw

"We smile when we see him, we laugh before he does anything; it makes us happy just to look at him."

— Pauline Kael

"He was one of the brightest stars in Hollywood, and his elegance, wit and charm will endure forever on film and in our hearts."

— Ronald Reagan

"His acting remains forever fixed in a time that never dates."

— Vincent Canby

"If you wanted to be happy you were going to see a Cary Grant movie."

— Ralph Lauren

[From his 1970 Honorary Oscar acceptance speech] "You know that I may never look at this without remembering the quiet patience of directors who were so kind to me, who were kind enough to put up with me more than once, some of them even three or four times. I trust they and all the other directors, writers and producers and my leading women have forgiven me for what I didn't know. You know that I've never been a joiner or a member of any particular social set, but I've been privileged to be a part of Hollywood's most glorious era."

— C.G.

"From Archie Leach to Cary Grant. What a giant step. And yet he became Cary Grant. He really became him."

— Deborah Kerr

An Invitation

With a view to future revisions, suggestions for additions, corrections of errors, or other changes are invited.

The publishers cordially invite you to submit your criticisms of this book and any other volumes that bear the History Company name. Ideas for new books or reprints to be added to our catalogue are also most welcome.

Please address your criticisms, corrections, or suggestions to: support@historycompany.com

www.ingramcontent.com/pod-product-compliance
Lightning Source LLC
Chambersburg PA
CBHW030928180526
45163CB00002B/497
9781492201397